A WORLD OF TREES

A Guide to the Importance of Trees

by Katherine E Lent

A World of Trees

Published by ➤ Rewind Design
Cincinnati OH USA

* * *

Forward

As a parent or educator, you likely want your children
to have an appreciation and respect for nature.

The aim of this book is to teach kids about
the importance of trees to the planet and all
of its' species through scientific fact,
historical reference and cultural insight.

I hope you will find this book a joy to read
with your children as you learn about a world of trees.

Two roads diverged in a wood, and I
- I took the one less traveled by, and
that has made all the difference.

~ Robert Frost

A World of Trees

CONTENTS

WE LIVE IN A WORLD OF TREES.

Trees are an important part of our world.

Trees and all of the species on Earth are partners. The air that we breathe in is what trees breathe out. Trees breathe in carbon dioxide and breathe out oxygen. Trees breathe in oxygen and breathe out carbon dioxide. We each keep the air clean and breathable for each other.

HEALTHY TREES, PEOPLE AND ANIMALS.

Trees help people and animals to stay healthy and keep us cool. They remove tons of carbon dioxide and air pollutants that are harmful to all life.

Trees produce foods like apples and nuts that feed people and animals. Their roots stop rain and rivers from runoff and flooding by absorbing excess water, reducing the amount of soil that's washed away into streams and lakes lessening erosion.

WHAT DOES THIS MEAN FOR YOU?

Part of the importance of trees is their practical benefits. The air that we breathe, the fruit that we eat, the paper that we write on and the homes that we build all come from trees.

Have you ever been so hot on a sunny day and stood under a tree to cool off? Animals do that too. We all need shade to shelter us from the hot sun. Have you ever picked fresh berries from a bush? Birds do that too.

Do you like to draw or paint on paper or read paper books? Now we have electronic tablets to draw on and read books on. Perhaps you are even reading this book on one! They help reduce the number of trees needed to cut down to make paper books.

Trees are the oldest living things on Earth.

Trees can live for thousands of years. An Aspen grove nicknamed 'Pando' in Utah shares a common root system and is over 80,000 years old and is the oldest known tree colony in the world.

Pando, (which is Latin for "I spread out"), also known as 'the trembling giant', is a clonal colony of an individual male *Quaking aspen (Populus tremuloides)*. It is located at Fishlake National Forest in Utah, United States.

The oldest known single tree is over 5,068 years old. *Pinus longaeva*, is among the longest-lived life forms on Earth.

'*Methuselah*' lives in the Ancient Bristlecone Pine Forest of the White Mountains in California. and is 4,850 years old. The locations of these cone-bearing conifers are kept a secret to protect them from vandalism.

PREHISTORIC TREE ANCESTORS.

The earliest trees were tree ferns, horsetails and lycophytes, which grew in ancient forests during the Carboniferous period; tree ferns still survive, but horsetails and lycophytes are now small plants. Prehistoric tree ferns are still around today. I have some in my yard!

Later, in the Triassic Period, conifers, ginkgos, and cycads appeared, and then flowering plants grew in the Cretaceous period. Most species of trees today are flowering plants and conifers. Ginko are still around today. You can find them on many NYC streets. They are my favorite tree!

HOW TREES LIVE.

Some trees can grow to over 300 feet or 100 meters in height. And that does not even include the roots that grow down into the earth! Trees that have their leave canopy down at ground level are called bushes and shrubs.

There are two main types of trees. *Deciduous* trees usually change color and lose all of their leaves in cold climates. They lose their leaves during the dry season in hot, dry climates.

Evergreen trees lose their leaves a little at a time with new ones growing in to replace the old so they stay green all year in every season. Trees can live in groups of different sizes. These groups are known as forests, groves, a wood or woods, an orchard, woodland, woodlot, thicket, savanna, rainforest or stand.

TREES IN OUR CULTURE.

The tree has always been a cultural symbol. Common icons are the *'World Tree'* and the *'Tree of Life'*. The tree is often used to represent nature or the environment itself.

Many societies throughout history have worshiped trees. Trees have played a very important role in many of the world's mythologies and religions, and have been given deep and sacred meanings throughout the ages.

TREES IN ART.

Trees are so often represented in all forms of art, from paintings to poetry, and in literature and even in songs. Look around your home and see if you can find any representations of trees. Some families put up an actual live cut evergreen for a Christmas tree.

If you look you will find representations of trees everywhere; on fabric patterns, jewelry and in architectural motifs. We adorn our shopping centers and residential neighborhoods with trees. *Egyptian columns had Papyrus motifs at the top.*

Have you ever been in the lobby of a hotel or big office building? If you look you will often find potted trees all around. You will often find potted trees in the *lobby of a hotel* or big office building.

ICONIC SYMBOLS.

Trees are easily recognizable iconic cultural symbols. Trees may represent our thought of and connection with nature.

Palm trees may make you think of the beach or the desert. *Evergreens* may make you think of cold and snow. *Deciduous trees* that change color may make you think of Autumn and holidays like Thanksgiving or Halloween.

THE SCIENCE OF TREES.

Trees are classified into many different 'orders' and 'families' of plants. They are given Latin and 'common' names. For example, you may have heard of an Oak tree but it's 'genus' name is *Quercus*, Latin for 'oak tree' of the beech family, *Fagaceae*. There are approximately 600 species of oaks.

We also use the common names to name the product that comes from them. You may have *Oak floors*, eat *Apples* or put *Maple syrup* on your pancakes.

Here are some well-known trees with their common, family and genus names.

- *Coconut, Genus: Coco*
- *Maple, Genus: Acer*
- *Oak, Genus: Quercus*
- *Pine, Genus: Pinus*
- *Willow, Genus: Salix*
- *Yew, Genus: Taxus*
- *Birch, Genus: Betula*

THE SCIENCE OF TREES.

The Roots grow underground with a few exceptions. The size of the root system is usually as big as the part of the tree above the ground. They keep the tree stable and collect water and nutrients from the soil to store them until needed.

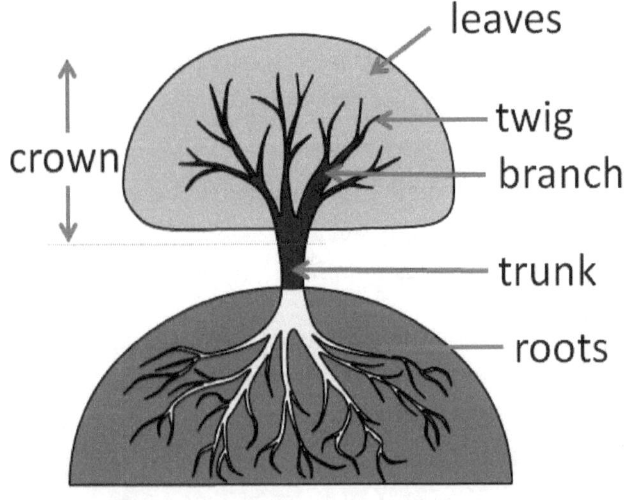

The *Mangrove tree*'s roots grow in water and the *Banyan tree* has aerial roots that grow above ground.

THE WOOD OF A TREE.

The **Branches** provide support and distribute the leaves efficiently and store water and nutrients, although most palm trees are not branched.

The **Trunk** support and holds up the crown. The trunk transports water and nutrients from the soil and sugar from the leaves.

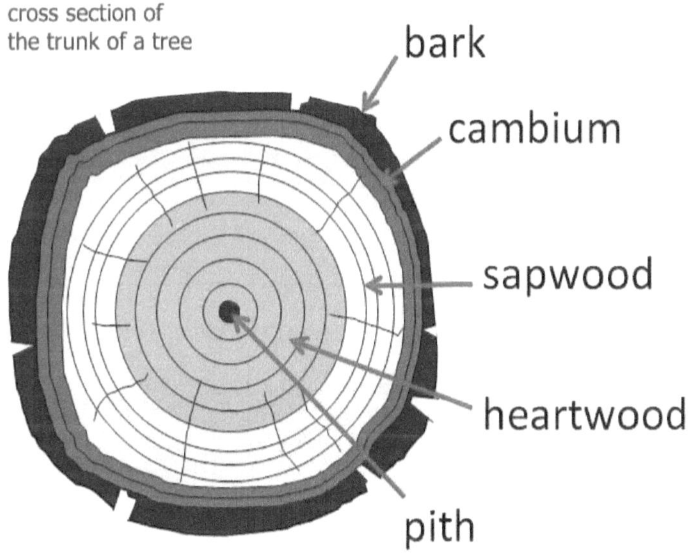

Inside the trunk of a tree, there are many Rings. A new ring is added for each year of the tree's life. The **Bark** is the outside layer of the trunk, branches, and twigs of trees.

The bark serves as a protective layer for the more delicate wood inside of the tree. Trees have **inner bark and outer bark** -- the inner layer of bark is made up of living cells and the outer layer is made of dead cells, sort of like our fingernails. There are some such as *Tree Ferns* that do not produce bark.

Sapwood is made up of a network of living cells that bring water and nutrients up from the roots. It is the youngest wood of the tree -- over the years, the inner layers of sapwood die and become heartwood.

The **Heartwood** is dead sapwood in the center of the trunk. It is the hardest wood of the tree giving it support and strength.

The **Pith**, (not to be confused with a pit), is the tiny sometimes dark spot of spongy living cells right in the center of the tree trunk.

Essential nutrients are carried up through the pith. Its' placement right in the center means it is the most protected from damage by insects, the wind or animals.

A WHOLE STORE IN A TREE.

You may be surprised how many products you use that come from trees! Many people think primarily about lumber and paper products when we think about products from trees.

Numerous products come from trees. Tree products vary from *food to building supplies to toys to instruments to packaging.*

Trees are of great economic value. They create consumer goods and jobs that fuel the economy in many different industries.

Products are another reason to manage our valuable *renewable* forests. The list below gives you an idea of how much our forests provide for us in the modern world.

Next time you explore the woods, take a moment to think of some things that trees supply.

Some products come from live trees, such as almonds, apples, bananas, and many fruits and nuts.

Some products from cut trees are solid wood made into lumber that is used to build homes, furniture, musical instruments, fences, and boats.

Products from wood pulp include paper for books, writing paper, copy paper, tissues, paper towels, and cardboard.

Products made from wood chips and sawdust are particleboard, plywood and garden mulch.

Products can also be made from Bark such as ceiling tiles, cork boards, subflooring, latex, cinnamon and some kinds of poisons.

Because the bark is a protective layer for the tree, it can keep itself safe from insects and animals. Strong flavors, scents, and toxins are used to make medicines from the bark of different types of trees.

BURNING WOOD CREATES ENERGY.

That energy is used to create the fuel to heat and to propel. Just that alone makes it extremely valuable as a *commodity*.

We can see why there are differing opinions about how to protect trees.

DAMAGE TO TREES.

Many dangers can befall trees. Trees are similar to people. Both can take a lot of some types of damage and survive, but even small amounts of certain types of trauma can cause death. Most people do not realize how easily a tree can be killed.

Tree damage comes from both living sources and non-living sources, and *deforestation*, the cutting down of trees.

Trees get diseases, insects bore into the bark, animals like deer, rub bark off the trunks, and vines and *fungi,* like *mushrooms*, can attach themselves to a tree.

Some countries will need to slow the rate of destruction. In some areas, they cut down *Palm trees* faster than they can replenish them.

They are valued for their *Palmetto* oil which helps their economy and provides jobs but it can destroy the animal habitat and their *ecosystem*. Tree management would help that process be more *sustainable*.

Non-living sources of damage can include *lightning, fire, storm winds, and construction activities*. People damage trees also. Some organizations understand the importance of tree health. *Tree management* helps protect the trees.

TREE APPRECIATION.

Most of all, it is important for us to understand the role that trees have in the world and the real partnership that we have.

Having that understanding makes it easy to appreciate all that trees have to offer and the beauty of experiencing trees in person, through one's work, through art, through travel and just through our everyday activities.

NEXT STEPS.

Start observing and enjoying trees on your route to school or home. Notice how different trees are used in parks, neighborhoods, and shopping areas.

These are activities that you can do easily, will become automatic, and will greatly deepen your enjoyment and appreciation of your relationship with trees.

- *Can you tell the difference between trees that are naturally occurring and those deliberately planted for beauty or function?*

- *Notice how trees look in different seasons and try to guess what their activities are.*

- *Are they setting up buds for the coming spring?*

- *Will they have flowers, fruit or seed pods?*

- *Do they drop their leaves or stay green through the winter?*

- *Try to identify them by their leaves and shape.*

- *What wildlife likes to live in those trees?*

- *Do you see birds, butterflies, and squirrels?*

MAKE UP YOUR OWN QUESTIONS!

About the Author.

Originally from New York, Katherine now lives in a log home in the woods. Her woods are filled with very tall deciduous trees that are native to Ohio such as *Sycamore, Ash, American beech, Ohio Buckeye, Silver maple, and Eastern hemlock.* Her favorite trees are *Gingko, Flowering cherry, and White birch.*

She has studied horticulture, landscape, floral and interior design. She loves writing, marketing and living in the woods, but her next home will be on a boat somewhere warm! Visit Katherine at her website, *katherinelent.com.*

BONUS CHAPTER: RESOURCES.

Updated links to resources that expand this book and other information can be found at katherinelent.com

- PLACES TO GO
- ACTIVITIES & PHOTOGRAPHY
- CAREERS
- EDUCATION
- CONSERVATION

PLACES TO GO

Going to special places designed specifically for the appreciation of trees can be a very special vacation, or just visit online. I have selected a few notable spots. Here are a few examples.

- The Ten Best Redwood Groves in California
- The Best Places to See Fall Foliage in the United States
- Remarkable Trees to See on Public Lands
- National Parks: Find a Park by State
- Directory of US and International Arboretums

ACTIVITIES

There are so many fun ways to learn about trees for any age. There are ideas for tree science investigations, literacy and math activities, book-related projects, and many terrific tree craft projects, tree art ideas to help you plan your tree activities, and some resources to have a nature walk at home or to host in your community.

- Free Activities for Kids
- Preschool Tree Activities
- Nature Walks

PHOTOGRAPHY

Start a hobby as a nature photographer. Get some tips for taking photographs of trees.

- Awesome Tree Photography Made Easy

CAREERS, EDUCATION & CONSERVATION

There are many types of jobs created because of the industry of producing things from trees, but there are also many professions where the work is done with the trees. There are some examples of careers working with or about trees and real-world examples of forestry-related jobs.

- Forestry and Natural Resources Lesson Plans
- US Forest Service
- 4H

WORLDWIDE CONSERVATION AND ENVIRONMENTAL ORGANIZATIONS

Lists of environmental organizations and exemplary sites promoting forest and woodland conservation.

* * *

Notes:

NOTES:

www.ingramcontent.com/pod-product-compliance
Lightning Source LLC
Chambersburg PA
CBHW031922270726
48655CB00007BA/3242